TERM LIMITS
AN EVOLUTIONARY FIX
FOR MARRIAGE

BY **BRAD BROWN**
WITH DAVE SHIELDS

Library of Congress Control Number: 2013935014
ISBN #: 9780989142731

Published by Stop the Presses, LLC
1827 Cottonwood Glen Court
Salt Lake City, UT 84117

Contents

For Katelyn, Carly, Lauren, Sabrina and children everywhere who have had no choice but to survive divorce.

As part of our effort to aid the children of divorce, a portion of the profits from this book are being donated to children's charities.

Introduction

When my marriage collapsed, it shattered me. I tried everything I could to save it for the sake of our children, but my wife had been living a secret life and the damage was beyond repair.

I'd never known I could hurt so badly, but it was about to get much worse because we had to tell the kids. That was the worst experience of my life. As excruciating as my pain had been, in comparison to theirs, it was nothing.

My seven year old asked me how I could give up on our family when I'd always told her never to give up on anything, not even chasing a soccer ball. I had no answer.

My ten year old asked nightly how I could live with my decision to ruin her life. As much as her words hurt, I couldn't blame her for her feelings. Still, there was no way to make her understand that this wasn't my choice.

My fifteen year old just sat in the corner of her closet and cried. When I tried to comfort her, she said, "Please go away." I could feel, woven into each girl's reaction, her overwhelming sense of betrayal, and I could also feel her love. I promised them that they were the most important thing in my world, that everything revolved around them, and that I would do whatever was in my power to make their lives the best they could be. I've never felt anything more comforting than the embraces that followed.

Unfortunately, I was about to learn yet another incredibly unpleasant lesson about divorce. Although I'd been an involved father, I wasn't the primary care provider. That meant I wasn't on equal footing when it came to child custody, and because the primary care provider is assumed to be in charge of the kids, the court also prefers that they get the house. Other details don't seem to matter. The evidence I'd collected was irrelevant. I was going to be forced to move out of my home and away from my children, even though I'd done nothing wrong. It seemed like too much to bear. My former lover had become the source of seemingly limitless misery. How could this be happening?

On one Saturday evening, after a string of difficult nights, I realized I wanted to talk to my old friend, Brad Brown. He always cheered me up because he lived life on his terms. Over the last few years of my marriage, I hadn't been doing that. The time had come to make a change.

It had been a long time since I'd seen Brad. I first met him when I was about ten years old. He tried to sneak into my house one night, intent on making out with my babysitter, who also happened to be his girlfriend. He was, instead, surprised by four kids who suddenly lost all their motivation to go to bed. For us, it was as if a movie star had jumped off the silver screen and into our living room. That night he became a legend, at least in my mind.

I didn't see him again until college where I discovered that he was a member of the top fraternity on campus. Everyone knew Brad. I decided to pledge, and when I was accepted, he became my Big Brother.

There was no one better to show me the ropes. He organized his own intramural athletic teams in both football and softball, ran for student body senate, sat on the university's academic policy advisory committee, was pledge trainer in the fraternity and attended practically every formal the Greek community offered. But what I always found amazing was that he did it all while working a full-time graveyard shift building industrial drill bits for oil rigs. His shift started at 11:00pm, ended at 7:30am, and he was at his first class starting at 8:50 a.m. His parents had put restrictions and conditions on helping him pay for college that didn't work for him, so Brad said, "Fine, I'll pay for it myself." And he did.

After he graduated, he moved out of state. It was a decade before I saw him again. It happened when, by pure coincidence, he had moved back into town with his new wife and accepted a job at the same small mortgage brokerage where I'd begun working only two months earlier. We had a great time working together, and enjoyed solving the world's problems in our spare time.

I eventually lost track of him again when I left the company. Shortly after that, he went through a divorce. That didn't seem to slow him down much. He opened up his own company and became quite successful. Meanwhile, I was swamped with career concerns, the birth of my first daughter and the completion of my first book.

Over the next fifteen years I only saw Brad a handful of times, but I was always envious of the clarity with which he continued to live his life. I'd fallen into a pattern of jumping through hoops to keep my wife happy. Meanwhile, he'd married another gorgeous woman. It stunned me when I learned his second marriage ended in divorce as well.

One thing was certain; Brad would have a unique perspective on my situation. So, depressed and confused about my failed marriage, I called him, not even sure if the phone number I had for him would still be good.

He answered on the first ring. "How are you, Buddy?"

"Lousy. Do you have plans tonight?"

"I do now. Where should we meet?"

A few hours later, I was telling Brad my story. When I finally finished, he said, "Sorry to sound callous, but I've heard this all before, many times. I've lived it myself… twice."

"I'm so miserable."

He nodded. "You're going to come out of this alright. Maybe better. Trust me. Just tell me when you're ready to hear the solution?"

I looked at him incredulously. "The solution?"

And then he turned on the charm. For the next hour, I listened in fascination as he laid out a preposterous, innovative, hysterical and brilliant plan for fixing the mangled institution of marriage in America. I laughed, I cried, I questioned, I agreed, and by the time he finished, I was sold.

"You need to put this in a book," I said.

"Okay, sure. But I haven't written much since college. Will you help me? I want to gift it to my daughter," he said.

I was already imagining giving copies to my own daughters. Each had recently said they'd never get married. The pain of divorce was just too great. I couldn't stand seeing them cut themselves off from what ought to be a wonderful relationship. I owed it to them to at least present this new idea.

I also knew the job would be cathartic, redemptive and transformative for me. It's as if this project found me in the moment I needed it most.

We shook hands and went to work. The result is this book, a unique story from a unique author with great perspective. I hope you find the ideas as entertaining and important as I do. I'm confident they will change lives for the better.

~ *Dave Shields*

The Stuff of Dreams

Mary was excited. She awoke with a smile and jumped out of bed. Even for just waking up she looked amazing. She paused by the mirror and smiled again. Not a hair out of place, and her nightgown with all the finest lace accentuated her sensational curves. She had the most expensive wardrobe for every occasion and was always happy. "Perfect again," she thought.

Servants attended to her every need and priceless gem-covered ornaments adorned her castle in the lush hillside overlooking the green valley below. She had everything anyone could ever want. She was a princess. She ate the finest, most wonderful meals, prepared by her royal chefs. She was loved by her adoring subjects and had traveled to every corner of her thousand mile kingdom, but today was going to be even better than all the others. Today was going to be special.

Today, she was to be married to Prince Archibald, the 3rd, a crown prince she had known her whole life. He was a noble knight – strong, handsome and fearless in battle. He was a complete gentleman who loved only her and was the picture of romance. He'd written her countless love letters and poetry. They enjoyed all the same things and were destined to be together. The marriage had been pre-arranged from birth by her loving royal parents, but it was one she fully desired. She had dreamed about this moment since she was old enough to remember.

It was a beautiful sunny day, and the entire kingdom would be out to participate in the celebration. She walked back across the rose petals that covered the floor of her chambers. She had to get ready. The ceremony was just a few hours away. Lying for a moment across the silk sheets on her royal bed, she gazed dreamily out her tower window that overlooked the forested hillside of her kingdom.

Taking it all in, she could hardly believe how perfect her life was.

Suddenly the bed began to shake and it grew dark in the room. The bed covers rose up in waves and gold-lined pillows bounced to the floor.

She heard voices and lay helplessly frozen with fear. Through the darkness she saw a figure emerging towards her with something in his arms...

"Archibald?"

"Get up, Mary," he said. "Patty needs her diaper changed, Emily wet the bed again and the twins are starving. I'm late for my tee time with the boys, so I'll see you in a few hours."

"Archie! You scared me to death!"

Now wide awake and looking at the identical twin boys jumping on her bed, she wished she could just slip back to her dreamland for even thirty more minutes.

Archie was a good man but certainly no royal prince, nor the picture of romance. Things weren't actually the way she envisioned they would be after the ceremony. They hadn't really seen eye to eye on the way the marriage was supposed to work. It had been almost two years since their last real date, and sex was virtually non-existent since the baby. It was a situation she was secretly grateful about.

She needed a break and just couldn't seem to get one. There were no servants to do her duties, and her cooking was far from royally wonderful.

A small hand tugged at her flannel pajamas. "Mommy, will you tell me a story?" Emily asked in her tiny little three-year-old voice.

"Alright, Sweetie, a quick one. I have a lot to get done today."

Emily looked devastated at not being the most important thing in her mother's life.

"Honey, you're Mommy's precious little princess. One day you'll grow up and meet a handsome prince, get married, build a beautiful castle on a hilltop, and live happily ever after."

Her voice trailed off and for a moment she was lost in thought. Damn, that's exactly what my mother told me. Fairytales and castles, she thought. Fairytales and castles...

REALITY SETS IN, AND THE REALITY IS THAT MARRIAGE IS NOT A FAIRYTALE.

Evolutionary Pressure

I believe in evolution. I believe that all things evolve. When a species fights for survival under the pressures of natural selection and survival of the fittest, it will evolve into an improved version of itself. What worked for it in the past does not in its current environment.

Unless it successfully evolves adaptations to the new conditions it faces, it simply goes extinct.

This perfectly describes the situation marriage is in right now. Compare the environment fifty years ago with the environment that you live in today. Think of all the things that have changed in our society over that time.

So much has happened. **Today's environment is drastically different from a generation ago, yet most people still cling to the hope that they can create a stable marriage under today's conditions using yesterday's model.** It's a recipe for disaster.

That's why marriage as an institution in America has failed. It's a mess. **Plagued with the empty realities and broken belief systems, it grows weaker by the day.** Millions are devastated by its false hope each year. The breakdown has become epidemic. Extinction is imminent.

This institution, like everything else on this planet, must evolve if there's any hope for its survival. The chaos that comes from an unhappy marriage ripples through every individual who knows or has contact with the couple. Their family, friends, neighbors and co-workers all suffer. Unhappy people do poorly at work. They are not as actively involved in their communities. Their hearts are heavy and their minds are laden with, "What happens if…" It's not that they aren't concerned with others or want to be negative, but they are often literally struggling just to make it through the day.

Who cares about global warming or being kind to a neighbor when your heart is broken?

How much can people give back to society when husbands and wives are at each other's throats and their children are suffering? Nothing else matters when the fighting and irreconcilable differences spill over into every aspect of people's everyday lives. We need **peace of mind** and the ability to **experience our dreams**, but we can't find them at home.

The fairytale is not reality.

Look at the facts. Think about your own life and count the number of broken relationships that have either directly or indirectly impacted you. If you don't have to start counting on your toes, consider yourself incredibly fortunate.

In the 2010 census, for the first time in history, fewer than 50% of the households in America were led by married couples, and the number continues to plummet.

What's going wrong?

It's time that we took an honest look at the problem

and figured out a solution. You don't get to *happily ever after* just because you got someone to say, "I do." It takes work over the life of your relationship. It requires a conscious effort to focus on satisfying the needs of your partner while also making sure that your own needs are being met.

It's about two people being happy,

Not Just One.

Succeeding at this mission could hardly be more important. The family is the building block of society. Fractured families have negative repercussions, all the way up and down the line.

15

Take a look at some recent divorce related statistics if you need proof of that statement:

- 75% of women applying for welfare benefits do so because of disrupted marriage or relationships.

- Broken families earn 42% less than intact families

  - This is worse than the Great Depression, where income contracted by only 30.5%.

- Children of divorce experience lower levels of educational achievement.

- In 1950, 12% of children were from broken families. In 1992, it had grown to 58% – an increase of 354%!

- Over $40 billion is paid out annually in spousal support. This does not include attorney fees.

- Of the few marriages that do last through time, an even smaller percentage of those are described as "happy" marriages.

The March, 2012, issue of *National Health Statistics Reports*, a publication put out by the U.S. Department of Health and Human Services, pointed out some dismal and alarming marital statistics:

- Over 50% of all **first** marriages end in divorce within twenty years.

- The statistics for second marriages are even worse.

- Barely 10% of marriages last over thirty years.

- The average life of all marriages is less than eight years.

- Men and women who cohabitate before getting married (whether engaged or not) are MORE likely to divorce versus those who don't.

- The percentage of partners who cohabit before marriage is steadily rising.

- Marriage as a percentage of the population is down.

- People with premarital children have a lower probability for successful marriages than people who don't have children prior to marriage.

- Children born outside marriage fare worse than those in married households.

- Proportions for premarital children are up to the highest level ever.

- Only 63% of children grow up in households with both of their biological parents, and that number is declining.

The report soberly *stated, "The statistics do not describe the probability that a first marriage will last a lifetime."*

Nowhere in this data-packed twenty-one page report is there a single statistic that would support the theory that marriage in America is a healthy institution.

Nothing they say gives any reason for hope on the horizon. The numbers are universally bad, and they are all getting worse.

It's time to face facts. The odds that you will have a happily-ever-after marriage that lasts a lifetime are almost non-existent.

One interesting note in this study, amidst all the negative depressing statistics, is that couples with the highest educations statistically had substantially the longest marriages. Although this subset is also moving in the wrong direction, it is doing better than the population as a whole. Maybe this has something to do with the main reason marriages fail... education/communication.

Maybe we ought to approach this situation like a college degree. Maybe we should become more educated about the person we are going to marry.

Hmmm.

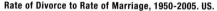

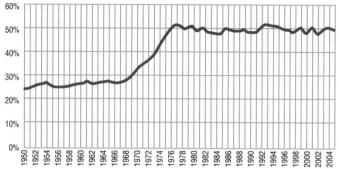

Rate of Divorce to Rate of Marriage, 1950-2005. US.

(Source: US Census Bureau. Statistical Abstracts of the United States, 2004-2005. "No. 70: Live Births, Deaths, Marriages, and Divorces: 1950-2002." Online www.census.gov/prod/2004pubs/04statab/vitstat.pdf. Center for Disease Control and Prevention, National Center for Health Statistics. National Vital Statistics Report, vol. 53, no. 21, Jun. 28, 2005, "Births, Marriages Divorce and Deaths," Table A, "Provisional Vital Statistics for the United States. "Online. www.cdc.gov/nches/data/nvsr/nvsr53/nvsr53_21.pdf)

The Quantum Shift

The graph above shows the rise in divorce rates. Things changed suddenly and drastically forty years ago. Social reform and modern thinking evolved in our society, but marriage remained unchanged and suffered because of it. The world is different now than it was then, and it's obviously not going back (nor should it).

If you're thinking about getting married, these stats might make you want to run for the hills. However, remember marriage doesn't start out that way. The wedding day is fun, and people tend to convince themselves that the statistics won't apply to them. At inception couples are positive and happy. Despite the odds, the fairytale persists, and for a **period of tim**e, all goes well.

That's because when people decide to get married, they are very optimistic and want to have a successful marriage. The magic is there and they start out with that warm, fuzzy notion it will last. They want to feel loved and want to be with that special "love of their lives." They believe in each other and feel secure and happy.

"THIS ONE IS A WINNER. I JUST KNOW IT!"

So why does the fairytale of marriage so often turn into such bitter disappointment? Why does it all fall apart? What happens that changes the optimism into dissolution?

While every divorce is unique, the causes of divorce are not. In nearly every instance, you will find some combination of the following ten problems:

1) Communication! This is the number one reason for divorce, but it's so cliché. Communication is not just talking, or listening. It's the conveying of a concept you hold in your head to another person who receives the data and holds the same understanding of the concept that you are trying to convey. It's not initially important to agree or respond, but more important to learn how to receive the concept to understand its implications.

Maybe we should rename the old cliché of "communication" to "education" in order to make it work.

Once we educate ourselves in communicating with our partners, we can truly understand what they want to achieve by being with us.

2) *Cheating and lies.* There's no place for these things in a healthy relationship. Deal killers every time.

The rest of the reasons for divorce are needs we all address and express at different levels. If you don't have problems with the first two things, the other issues that follow can be worked through, in most instances:

3) Money

4) Unmet expectations

5) Religion

6) Sex

7) Society and work

8) Mid-life crises

9) Addictions

10) Little things that add up

Look over this list. **These are not earth shattering marital complications that just came out of some new study.** These are things you should have already known about. What is earth shattering, then, is that **nobody does anything preemptively to address these issues**. We all know these things are important when we decide to get married, so why not address them in advance?

Now, think about marriage. You make vows and promises to your spouse. It's literally a contract, and if you think it isn't, you're wrong. You enter into an agreement with someone you love and make a bunch of promises, but mostly you have no basis for execution or performance. There are no provisions in marriage established to rectify any of the situations on the previous page, should there be problems.

"I JUST SIGNED ON THE DOTTED LINE, AND I HAVE NO IDEA WHAT IT MEANS."

Hey, you're married, "Till death do us part." The contract is for life with no way out other than death or divorce. Now figure it out... for better or worse, right? So why doesn't it address your needs and clearly explain your role in the partnership?

Why isn't it written in a way so that when you say **"I do,"** you know exactly what that means?

"WHAT ARE MY DELIVERABLES? EXPECTATIONS?
WHAT DO I GET IN RETURN?
I'M SURE THERE ARE PERFORMANCE BONUSES... RIGHT?"

Ironically, the reality is that today's marriage contract is so abstract you can't even get a good definition in a dictionary.

mar·riage
[mar·ij]

-noun

1. legal union of a man and woman
2. similar union involving partners of the same gender
3. wedding
4. any close association or blending of different elements

It's so vague and relative to each person's interpretation, it's become absurd. It should be binding and specific, like any other contract, but it isn't. So many people seem to view marriage as little more than a description of their current social standing or a method to gain tax benefits and insurance considerations.

Lots of married people continue to behave as though they are still single. Many are in it for what they can get out of it for themselves and couldn't care less how they perform for their partners. Many people marry, completely aware they will not honor their vows or keep their promises long term.

The bottom line is, saying you're married doesn't carry the ramifications that go with most contracts, even though it should be more important than the other commitments you make. In the minds of many people, marriage is not respected or upheld like a normal contract. Many people will honor a car payment longer than they'll stay married... and they are far more concerned about the repercussions of breaching those terms.

WHY?

Society went through a transformation. Viewpoints were altered as women entered the work force and equal rights prevailed. With societal changes came intense pressure on the entire system. Divorce rates rose dramatically as couples' needs shifted from just a few decades before. As people demanded change to the current model, lawmakers came up with a plan to fix the institution of marriage. They gave us no-fault divorce as their answer to the problems plaguing America's families. Boy, brilliant. That's the height of stupidity.

They didn't strengthen marriage, they sanctified divorce!

In doing so, they ran away from the real problem and created a multi-billion dollar industry *with divorce attorneys as the master of ceremonies.* Their actions further undermined the very institution they'd been tasked to fix.

The result? Either party can now end the marriage contract at any time, and for any reason. In fact, they don't even need to cite a reason! Getting divorced is easy... maybe expensive, damaging, and often life altering for the one getting jilted... but easy.

The cold hard fact is, thanks to no-fault, as far as the courts are concerned, marriage vows are now meaningless when it comes to getting divorced. Your certificate is just a nice piece of paper with your signatures on it. As much as marriage might mean to you, emotionally, spiritually, morally, or in any other way, if you ever find yourself faced with divorce, you will soon discover that the strength of your contract was based on only one thing, and that was the **willingness** of you and your spouse to abide by it.

Once either party decides they want out, the marriage contract essentially ceases to be binding.

No-Fault Divorce

Faced with a massive backlog of contested divorce cases in the late 60's, the state of California came up with an innovative solution. They eliminated the requirement for providing cause. If either party wanted out of a marriage, there was no longer anything to contest. Marriage became the only contract where the promises made at signing don't matter.

Impressed by the efficiency of this idea, the other 49 states followed suit within the next two decades.

Yeah, it was "for life" yesterday. Tomorrow, it can be terminated. Unlike legal actions brought about as a result of enforceable contracts, any evidence you collect to demonstrate why your marriage failed is essentially irrelevant.

No business would ever enter into a contract under such terms. What's the point of having a contract in place at all if it will cease to exist the moment a dispute arises? *No CEO worth their salary would ever sign on that dotted line.*

With no defined benefits, consequences, or stipulations for performance, and no penalties for broken promises, the contract becomes little more than a pie-in-the-sky, hope-it-works-out-for-the-best, agreement.

Think about marriage. Is there something exceptional about this particular sort of union that would dictate that, unlike any other partnership, it's impossible for it to be defined by an enforceable contract? Of course not. As a matter of fact, there's a common type of contract that's used within the marriage relationship in order to **clearly define** matters that most married couples do not define in advance. Unfortunately, these contracts are most often used when one party wants to protect something of value that they believe they are bringing to the marriage. These contracts, of course, are known as prenuptial agreements. Properly written, they are easily enforceable.

However, ask your friends and family what they think of a prenuptial, and you're likely to discover that most people see them as a contract that would never be put in place if not for the expectation that they will eventually be negatively enforced. In other

"THIS PRE-NUP IS GOOD FOR OUR FUTURE. AFTER ALL, IT'S HEALTHY FOR OUR LAWYERS TO START DEVELOPING A RELATIONSHIP."

words, a pre-nup is perceived by many to be the groundwork for a coming divorce. Because traditionally most productive relationships are ultimately based on trust and not paperwork, this sort of a contract can have the unfortunate effect of weakening a marriage before it even begins.

31

Mom and Dad Did It

I grew up believing in marriage. After all, my parents have been married for over fifty years. They would always talk about the day of my marriage. You know, the day I found that, "one and only." The day I permanently tied my future to the girl who was born to be my special mate *for life*.

I heard again and again about that fateful event and how my destiny would be realized as I took on life's ups and downs with my partner. The catch phrase was always, "Once you get married,…" you'll have this thing or that thing. "Once you find that special girl, you'll just know." "Once you get married, you'll see what we're talking about." "Once you get married, you'll know more about life." "Once you get married,…" etc., etc., etc.

I waited with anticipation, knowing my happily-ever-after was sure to come. I was searching, dating, and learning about love… until one day, at the age of thirty, I felt I'd finally found "THE ONE."

Yay!!!

Funny thing! What no one ever mentions a single word about is …

DIVORCE!

Boy, if that's not a buzz kill. Wish I'd had a bit more prep work on that one. Weird. Ignorance is NOT bliss… unless you can carry it off for life!

A Thriving American Industry: Divorce
The average divorce in America costs about $15,000 per spouse. With over a million divorces a year, this equates to a $30 billion dollar industry! That's money that loving couples saved up together, then set fire to in an attempt to destroy each other's lives. What a pathetic waste.

Remember, if your marriage eventually falls apart, you probably won't be the only ones who will pay the price.

35

Going through divorce shatters one's old belief systems about being married. It's quite a betrayal from the idea of becoming a member of the institution in the first place.

I've since come to think of our current marriage system a lot like believing in Santa Claus. It's all magical and wonderful at first. You can't wait for Santa to come, and you dream of all the great things he will bring you. Then one day, you find out it's all an elaborate fabrication. It's not true. There is no Santa Claus!

How could this be? The devastation does more than just shatter your beliefs! Good grief, the very people I trusted the most pulled this over on me. "Thanks, Mom and Dad."

It's worse if you're one of those kids who believed until the bitter end. You know, the one the other kids poked fun at and said, "He still believes in Santa."

I think Santa is all good and great, but geez, after a certain age let's cough up the truth! Right?

Well, let me tell you, the stories we grow up with about marriage and Santa are interchangeable.

The magic and fairytale of marriage ends pretty damn fast when it all falls apart in divorce court.

People who've been through a divorce often speak in a mocking tone about those who are starting their first marriage. "Oh, they still believe in the fairytale. How cute." People poke fun at marriage much like they did with the kid who still believed in Santa until the bitter end. Again, I love the idea of the magical love-at-first-sight romances that last forever and all, but I think we need to be realistic and temper the fairytale a bit. Cough up the truth before we enter into this, blindly believing that everything is destined to work out. Seriously, I think we need to know the pitfalls and risks that no one talks about... beforehand!

As parents we need to prepare our children to have healthy relationships and explain that marriage is never automatically happily ever after, nor is it a fairytale that just happens.

Not only does it take a lot of work, but it also takes realistic discovery about the person you're getting hitched to. Are they really who they say they are, and who they have led you to believe they are? Are you both on the same page with your expectations for this union and your commitment to making it work? Do everything possible to find this out beforehand, because finding it out after the fact will be painful.

Even the best prepared – people with honest intentions and the willingness to make all of the required sacrifices – sometimes fall into the trap. That's because there are some pretty self-serving manipulative people out there, and they're really good at deception. Some of them are deceiving themselves along with everybody else.

With that in mind, let me point out one thing and make a suggestion:

Not every marriage ought to survive, and not everyone should get married.

This flies in the face of traditionalist thought. After all, isn't marriage supposed to be for life? Maybe even for all eternity? But let's take a look at your lifestyle. Maybe you've never committed to anyone or anything for more than a few months. Then…

Wham!

Suddenly you meet the person of your dreams! So now you think you can just get married and give 100% with full commitment for life?

"Till death do you part."

Really? Given your track record, do you seriously believe you're capable of a commitment of that magnitude? Current marriage contracts accept only "life" commitments, so do you feel positive that when you stand in front of everyone and make that vow, you're really prepared to live up to your promise?

Are you being honest with yourself and your mate?

Let's set this thing up so we're likely to succeed, not certain to fail.

When you think you're ready to spend a lifetime with someone, be realistic. Romance and love can be blinding, and there are many types of relationships that don't (or shouldn't) lead to marriage.

Take a step back and make sure this is a relationship you could imagine being in for life.

The reality is that not every crush you have is going to have potential lifetime staying power.

Learning how to be in a loving relationship takes time and commitment (as well as trial and error), so maybe you need to practice at a few relationships before you dive in. Maybe you're the type that gets bored quickly, or you just develop that seven year itch at seven months.

So it's as much about knowing yourself as anything.

Now That You're Ready

Ultimately when you really think you're ready and start talking to your partner about marriage, that's when you need to get really serious about the concepts here.

There may be a better way to get where you dream of going than by following a pathway that's led to failure for the majority of the people who've traveled it ahead of you.

First of all, why are you getting married? Seriously, what's the real reason you're doing it? Are you looking for that fifty year love that never dies and lasts a lifetime? Or are you just trying to pacify your partner? Does marriage mean ownership to you? Is it security? Be brutally honest with yourself and list the exact reasons. Every one of them.

Take a moment right now to write them down. Figure out what in the world it is that you are expecting to get from this relationship:

My reasons for getting married:

In five years, will your list still be the same? There's a really good chance it won't.

Maybe your reasons for getting married are for love, or maybe all you're really after is a healthy sex life. Fun times with a fun partner may be all you need, or maybe you feel money can literally make a person you have limited physical desire for suddenly become a very *attractive* option. If those are your true feelings, then it's okay to have them, but YOU NEED TO SAY IT!

A person has a right to know why you're with them.

"HEY BILL, REMIND ME WHY WE MARRIED?"

"YOU WANTED THE ARTS SECTION."

Two people are never going to marry for exactly the same reasons. Your partner might have motivations for being with you that you can't entirely relate to, but that's okay. The bottom line is, once the truth is known and you both <u>agree</u> to be together, you get to figure out how to fit it all into the context of a mutually working relationship.

Then also understand we all need ***peace of mind***, and that comes from a little pre-planning. It's comforting to know what you can expect and what is expected of you beforehand. Maybe the reality is that no matter what you do in your relationship it will ultimately end with a parting of the ways. Maybe that relationship really **should** end, and hanging on is unhealthy. Let's say you both really tried. It's possible your needs can never be met with the person you are currently with.

Wouldn't that knowledge be extremely valuable and wouldn't it be far better and more amicable if you knew what to expect when things ended?

Wouldn't it be better if, along the way, you knew exactly what you were supposed to be doing to make things work? Wouldn't it be better to know how your affairs were going to be handled ahead of time instead of the ginormous slap in the face at divorce court?

Of course!

So this is where you get to go to school to learn how to do it. Your education/communication begins with hands on training between you and your partner. How can you measure performance if there's nothing stating what it should be? Your marriage certificate doesn't tell you, and it doesn't come with instructions.

It's critical both partners define their expectations.

People spend four years or more in college educating themselves to get a better job, but...

THEY SPEND VIRTUALLY NOTHING PREPARING TO HAVE AN ENRICHING RELATIONSHIP WITH THE PERSON THEY PLAN TO MARRY.

They spend even less time figuring out what to do if, by chance, things don't work out.

It's time to earn a degree in your lover!
Fortunately, home study courses are available.

By the way, I don't think there's any couple that can't be together, no matter their race, religion, social status or anything else. As long as they have three things:

1) Attraction strong enough to call love, which results in desire and spending quality time together.

2) Willingness to continue to work at and improve the relationship and satisfy each other's needs. Education and communication are the keys here.

3) Honesty that is absolute when dealing with one another. Not just telling the truth, but being the true you. You must show respect for each other through truthfulness in order to develop real trust and commitment.

Wow!
Term Limits

In 2000, I was watching the presidential elections. A bunch of friends and I were talking about congressmen and senators and their lack of term limits. We were discussing how long they'd been in office when, in fact, they had only two to six year terms before facing re-election. Despite this, most of these officials had been in office for decades. They were career politicians. I made a joke that these guys had terms that far exceeded most marriages in the United States.

Wow, now that's pathetic.

But then I thought about it. Every election, we as voters exercise our choice to *renew* and put those people back in Washington to represent us. We decide as voters! Around election time our officials really start putting out to get our votes. They are definitely on their best behavior, and if they can sway us to re-elect them, then why not? If they're wrong for the job, we vote them out and move on. Too bad we can't have a renewal term to do the same with marriage, I thought. Boy, would things be different.

"Okay, Bob, yes I will marry you, but under one condition! We write up the terms and then we get four years to prove it will work. I'll even throw in the first option to renew."

That's the basic idea of Term Limits... marriage structured to work within a realistic time frame.

"HEY MARGE, DID YOU REALIZE OUR MARRIAGE CONTRACT INCLUDES THE FIRST OPTION TO RENEW?"

Maybe it doesn't seem very romantic, but hey, it's real! It's definitely far more romantic than divorce. The life contract the government currently forces you to make, in order to have a recognized marriage, is an undefined, poorly executed contract that needs to have options. With the Term Limits contract a couple starts with serious discussions about the issues that matter most to them, and then they draw up a working agreement with each other, based upon their discoveries.

An interesting point needs to be made here. Since divorce rates skyrocketed in the 70's, many social workers and others have sought the answers to the modern problems facing couples and marriage. There are times when part of the problem has been addressed, but never the whole thing at once. They all seem to focus on different stages of the relationship but fail to implement an ongoing fix. In the process they have created some useful tools.

Here are some examples:

1) Compatibility tests for matchmaking

2) Prenups to predetermine dividing the assets in a divorce

3) Contracts that clearly define relationships between two parties

4) Counseling assistance for working through and enriching your relationship

5) Tax incentives to strengthen families

Term Limits takes the best of these concepts and pulls them together into a working contract that has been missing until now.

It's actually quite simple, and mostly just a matter of rearranging the very same pieces into a more effective order while attaching the key element of a time limit to evaluate performance.

Ultimately it might be one of those situations where the solution is so obvious that everybody just overlooked it.

Take a close look at the two columns below for a better understanding of the rearrangement I'm referring to:

Comparison of Marriage Alternatives

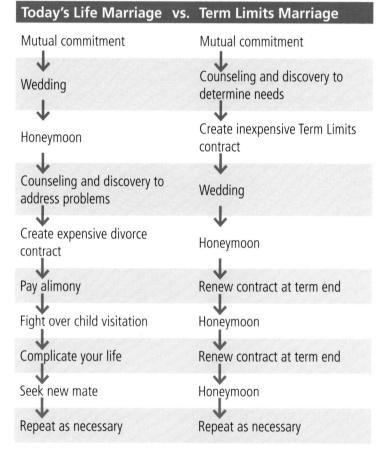

Today's Life Marriage	vs.	Term Limits Marriage
Mutual commitment		Mutual commitment
↓		↓
Wedding		Counseling and discovery to determine needs
↓		↓
Honeymoon		Create inexpensive Term Limits contract
↓		↓
Counseling and discovery to address problems		Wedding
↓		↓
Create expensive divorce contract		Honeymoon
↓		↓
Pay alimony		Renew contract at term end
↓		↓
Fight over child visitation		Honeymoon
↓		↓
Complicate your life		Renew contract at term end
↓		↓
Seek new mate		Honeymoon
↓		↓
Repeat as necessary		Repeat as necessary

Installing each component properly dramatically improves the outcome.

Let's dig just a little bit deeper into each of the steps mentioned in the chart from a Term Limits perspective.

1) *Mutual commitment* – It doesn't matter how you met your mate or why you're attracted to each other. All that matters is that you've both decided that it's time to take dating to the next step. So at this point you are probably either engaged or seriously considering becoming engaged.

Key components:

- You're feeling sure you want this thing to last and make a long term commitment.

2) *Counseling and discovery* – This is the communication phase, and it is the most critical step of the process. It's pretty simple stuff, but it rarely gets done. Using tools I call "discovery tools," you educate yourself in understanding what your partner needs from you in the relationship. They tell you what YOU will be required to give them and what they are willing to give to you in return. You tell them what you need from THEM and what they will be required to give you. If there's agreement, you can move on.

Key components:

- Establish mutual needs and benefits for being together with "discovery tools" – questionnaires that identify and discover why you are attracted to each other, what each of you needs from the other, and the things you are expecting to experience from being together.

- Write it down. Put in writing the needs each of you has, clearly defining what you are expecting. Write down how those needs will be fulfilled.

- Discuss points of contention. Anything you discover that may lead to future problems needs to be handled here. Talk to a counselor, if needed, to make compromises until you reach agreement.

Notice that I'm not suggesting anyone *change* themselves. This is about communicating who you are and what you need, not altering it. It's critical for people to tell their mates exactly what

"WHAT ARE YOU TALKING ABOUT? THIS IS JUST HOW I AM."

"PERHAPS, BUT WE CAN CHANGE THAT."

they're about so they can **accept** each other for who they are and move forward based on that.

Counseling at this phase is used for guidance and to *create!* At this stage both people are optimistically working together. After problems arise or at the divorce stage, counseling is more likely to become a tool of justification and destruction.

3) *Create inexpensive Term Limits contract* – In this step you put together a contract on which you both agree. It includes written duties, performance measurements and consequences for breach, all based upon your discoveries in the previous step. This contract actually specifies **in writing** what each person's reasons are for being with their partner, what their needs are that must be met by their partner, what they hope to experience from being with their partner, and for **how long** they both agree to abide by the contract. **Let me emphasize, the *time limit* is clearly set.**

For each of the items in the contract there must be a specific and detailed list of agreed upon penalties and consequences for breach. Unlike traditional marriage documents, it's the sort of contract that a businessperson would actually consider signing. This contract then becomes part of the marriage agreement.

Key components:

- A written signed document notarized and drawn up by an attorney that clearly states everything above.

- The contract outlines a time limit for evaluation. This is agreed to by the couple, so that during this time they can expect to receive the benefits promised by their mates.

- Predetermined ending with division of all assets, in case the union becomes dissolved.

- Consequences that the couple establishes at inception (like early termination fee or breach of fidelity penalty)

"WHAT DO YOU MEAN THERE'S AN EARLY TERMINATION FEE?"

4) *Wedding* – At this point it's time to really
celebrate… not just getting married, but to celebrate your partner and all you have accomplished together to get here. This is the true expression of the promises you made to each other. It's not just a ceremony saying, "Hey everyone, we want to be together!" It's saying we have put in place the things to make it work and last.

Key components:

- True celebration of a work in progress.

5) *Honeymoon* – This is a great tradition
that now has more meaning and will be more enjoyable. There's peace of mind that you are both starting out on the right track, removing a lot of the worries about the future and allowing you to more fully enjoy this needed break. There's also the comfort of knowing, if you continue to meet each other's needs, you will both be much more likely to want to renew and stay together. This tradition can last throughout your marriage, expressed again and again each time you renew, rather than just for a few days after the initial ceremony like in the past.

Key components:

- Since you and your mate have worked

through your expectations for being together, there is more comfort and peace of mind looking forward, making this needed break more rewarding.

- This tradition can be celebrated again and again, each time you renew.

6) *Renew contract at term end*

– If you had a good marriage for the first term, you redefine your new terms and renew. Renewal is always EARNED and mutually agreed upon, but not guaranteed. This is ultimately where performance for your actions and keeping your promises is evaluated.

Key components:

- Evaluation of promises made and needs fulfilled.

- If the couple agrees they have had a successful experience, they renew their commitments for the next term and repeat the previous five steps... including full celebration.

- If the union has been a bad experience, the couple falls back to the predetermined dissolution agreement they created under their contract in step three.

Relationships...
Defined

Understanding the concepts in greater detail...

Undefined relationships are exactly what we have in society now. At best, we have a verbal or assumed set of rules we hope our partners abide by when we get married. Their willingness to do so is all we have to fall back on. So except for the pie-in-the-sky loose set of assumed behaviors, marriage is basically **undefined**.

What we need are DEFINED RELATIONSHIPS with *defined parameters* and *terms.*

Maybe we need to think in smaller steps and work in the here and now on a daily basis to achieve "marriage." In other words, we define our wants and needs, agree to give each other the things necessary to have an enriching experience **together** in a committed relationship for a specified number of years, and then redefine those needs at the end of the term. Doing this over and over, a couple can truthfully say they have a "marriage."

Additionally, once you have full knowledge and agreement to be together, and you are working to do your part in satisfying the needs of your partner, the reasons you stay together may be completely different from what your reasons were for getting together originally.

ONE THING WE CAN COUNT ON IS THAT WE CAN'T COUNT ON MUCH OF ANYTHING... EXCEPT THAT EVERYTHING CHANGES.

Things change, yet with upfront ongoing education/ communication, the dynamics fall into place based on a foundation of truth. Things **evolve** and grow into a reality that couldn't possibly be formed from the base of deception or misunderstanding that is often the case in a loosely undefined marriage. Hey, relationships with honesty and trust and **defined benefits** are extremely attractive and rewarding.

So you met THE ONE and now you're ready to share your life with them? Pull your head out of the clouds for a brief moment. Put the fairytale aside and get down to the meat of your union. Forget about planning the wedding or the honeymoon and concentrate on making plans for your life together. Make it work now, and your honeymoon will last the throughout the rest of your relationship.

Fight now, honeymoon later.

Write down your terms. Sit down with your partner and work out a **defined** Term Limits contract. The contract will identify your wants and desires as well as your partner's. You educate each other while communicating your expectations for a relationship that will exist over a specified term. It is a performance based agreement. Term Limits is a way of interacting with your partner to achieve success at having a more enriching relationship for **the time** you are together.

Term Limits is a contract that has an ENDING! Term Limits is an agreement to achieve success in a relationship through a mutually beneficial, pre-determined exchange of needs between partners for an agreed upon amount of time. It includes enforceable consequences.

Take a moment to compare the Term Limits description of marriage above, to the definition of a traditional marriage below, as mentioned earlier:

mar·riage
[mar-ij]
-noun

1. legal union of a man and woman
2. similar union involving partners of the same gender
3. wedding
4. any close association or blending of different elements

Which would you rather have?

If successful, a Term Limits marriage can, and hopefully will, be RENEWED indefinitely! Both parties in a partnership need to communicate and re-focus at regular intervals. Term Limits achieves that.

It creates a perfect environment for couples to stand on equal footing as they redefine their needs, desires and commitment to each other.

Is that spark that made the relationship exciting still there after five years? What can I do to make the next five years even better?

The key is to ask and answer probing questions. Why did you both get together in the first place? WHAT IS IT ABOUT ME THAT ATTRACTS YOU? What is it that you want to experience with each other? How long do you want to be together to experience it? What are your goals for the future? What are your personal ambitions? What do you need from your partner? What does your partner need? Can you honestly give it to them? WRITE IT ALL DOWN!

If you could use some assistance figuring out what ought to be on this list, go to www.TermLimitsMarriage.com and take advantage of the free, interactive discovery tools.

IT ISN'T AS HARD TO BE HAPPY AS YOU'RE MAKING IT!

By taking this marriage thing in smaller steps and working in the here and now every day, we might have the best shot at achieving long-term goals.

Term Limits can literally be hands-on higher education to earn a rewarding degree in the marriage experience.

Knowing your partner and knowing your expectations while getting back the benefits you seek, helps your relationship grow and improve with each subsequent term.

In essence you renew because it's satisfying, and you'll be extending the honeymoon every time you renew.

JUST TAKE A MINUTE AND THINK ABOUT IT!

Look, you're going to get married anyway, right? I mean, you're at that point. It's romantic and fun and exciting. But have you thought about how ugly it could get? **You need to, because things don't end pretty or they would never end at all**. The statistics show pretty beginnings have ugly endings all too often. If they're going to end ugly, at least be prepared so that it's not uglier than it needs to be.

Remember, no matter what, when one person has lost sight of their commitment to the other, everything can unravel fast. Either an undefined relationship (like marriages are currently) or a **defined relationship** (the kind I propose) can and will end. There is no surefire guarantee to avoid things falling apart. However if there are defined parameters and defined consequences for the ending, at least some of the damage can be mitigated.

Surely defined Term Limits would be preferable to the who-knows-what-will-happen chaos of an undefined marriage and divorce. Plus, because of the pre-agreed to **consequences**, there's motivation to at least see the original agreement to the end. This gives partners time to make adjustments and new plans in the event that things don't work out. That's miles ahead of the undefined marriage in which you file for divorce and bring out the heavy artillery.

In a defined agreement you already know how it's going to end if things fall apart. It's still sad for the person who wants to continue, but ultimately it provides the basis for a more amicable separation and some peace of mind for both partners. **Even more importantly, you both have a written plan for making the relationship succeed by satisfying each other's needs.** You actually get to **start out with a map** and a set of critical guidelines that will point you toward success. Isn't that extra effort up front worth avoiding becoming embroiled in a bitter divorce?

So maybe you're thinking, "Why not just write a prenuptial contract as standard procedure for every person getting married? Why have Term Limits?"

"ARRGHHH! NOW TAKE YEE TEN PACES WEST AND DIG..."

The answer is because a Term Limits contract would offer so much more. For one thing, it enables us to put a time limit on one another to evaluate performance. **We don't really have a lifetime to figure out if we're in the right relationship.** We need to know sooner rather than later, and the pressure of a deadline will often make that possible.

It comes down to intent and honesty. A prenup can be seen as a back door escape clause, or even a pre-determined intent to fail. With Term Limits both parties are basically in an agreement to *provide* specific things their partners *need*, and they promise to do it for the specified term, in order to SUCCEED. They both know the specific tasks they have agreed to perform, and they know the consequences if they don't do their part.

Also, Term Limits are just that: **Limits**. There is a very real foreseeable **end** to the contract. If both parties don't agree it works after the designated term is up, it's over.

So the difference between Term Limits and prenuptial marriage is this: Term Limits is a working contract that both parties agree to actively participate in, with each agreeing to fulfill a predetermined list of needs for their partner while getting their own needs met. It's generally more specific than a prenuptial.

Term Limits is built around a working attitude toward success rather than a pre-acknowledged division of assets upon failure.

This new plan shares the fundamental characteristics of prenuptial marriages with a few major differences.

1) Term Limits defines in writing why the partners have chosen to join in marriage and what they need to get out of the relationship.

2) Term Limits includes an expiration date which defines how long the agreement is to be upheld.

3) Term Limits gives both parties an opportunity to redefine their needs and renew the contract at regular intervals, thus making for:

An ongoing work in progress.

Isn't this ultimately what a marriage should be?

As you are probably starting to see, the individual components of Term Limits strengthen the whole as you fit them together. Because everything is built upon a foundation of honesty, actions designed to accomplish one thing end up having several positive side effects. For instance, the short term nature of the contract, which was designed to transform the marriage promise into something that the modern couple actually has a hope of accomplishing, has the pleasant benefit of creating an environment where both parties would automatically work toward earning a contract extension, thereby increasing the strength and duration of the marriage.

Motivation is strengthened by participation!

The whole becomes greater than the sum of its parts.

Term Limits Applied

Imagine if Term Limits contracts were applied to the institution of marriage. Sure, it might seem a little strange compared to the way things are now, but it's real and has function.

Since the system that's currently in place has failed so miserably for the last fifty years and continues to get worse, it's pretty obvious it needs to evolve yet again into something better. We have to rethink the way we marry, just as people have done all through time?

For example, this is how silly things are now in the US. I have a friend whose been dating this girl for two years. He's crazy about her, and they clearly enjoy doing everything together. I've gotten to know her through him, and I think she's great. So one day I asked him what he was going to do... get married, move in together or keep dating? His answer was classic. He told me, quite reluctantly, he'd probably be engaged within the next few months.

When I teased him about his discomfort he told me he'd seen many promising marriages fail, and he didn't want to join that sad crowd. He was really having trouble with it. It scared him. The problem isn't commitment, because he is completely committed. He really wants to do something, but he hates the whole idea of marriage/divorce.

"After all," he said, "maybe our fantastic swinging-from-the-chandeliers sex will become a thing of the past on the day we get married. We have fun now, so why ruin that? At least not for a while longer."

Wow! You hear that all the time. "Why ruin a good thing by getting married?" People are afraid to get married. They look at it as a job. It's no fun. It's the day they get stuck with the ball and chain.

This feeling permeates a general feeling in society. People don't see it as improving their relationship because, quite honestly, there's nothing on that piece of paper that identifies any way it will.

Obviously my friend isn't alone. Like many others, he doesn't really think marriage will be fun. He may even subconsciously feel she's only so exciting to be with now because she's trying to get him to sign on the dotted line for life. And his statements reveal that he believes marriage is definitely going to change all that... for the worse.

So what's wrong with saying that to his girlfriend and telling her his needs and expectations? What's wrong with putting that in writing?

SPIT IT OUT!

Her side of the story is a little different. She really loves him and wants to spend her life with him. Eventually she even wants children. But her fear is that he'll never settle down and provide the sort of environment he claims he's capable of. She wants the security of a certain level of income, and she's uncomfortable just rolling the dice on a lifetime decision in hopes that he'll fulfill his promise.

Is there any benefit to her getting married and eventually being disappointed? Why not put it in writing and express to him what her needs are in order to be happy. She should tell him everything she'll need from him, in order to give back to him what he needs.

What if, before they signed their names to the marriage document, they sat down with each other and sincerely figured out what they really wanted out of their relationship, and then put it on paper. Together they could strike up a document that, unlike a marriage certificate, actually measured their performance in upholding their commitments to each other,

77

and they could impose a time frame that had to be adhered to. No more waiting a lifetime to find out if someday the vows would be realized and the promises fulfilled.

If they executed this agreement before they got married, do you think there's any reason to believe their relationship would play out differently than if they just rolled the dice and got married without it?

So being specific on what's important for each individual is critical and leads to better interaction with fewer disagreements. Put down what you believe is needed in your contract. Talk about and identify real concerns and things that are rarely discussed before marriage commitments are made. Discuss everything, even the stuff that's uncomfortable. You're shooting for total discovery here. Holding back and being reserved defeats the whole purpose of getting educated and communicating with your partner.

I know it's hard to have complete disclosure, but this is critical.

"Yeah, but I'm shy and it's hard to talk about my feelings."

GET OVER IT!

You'll definitely have to talk about them in divorce court. Make sure you deal with every topic that's important to either of you. For example, there's a three letter word that start's with "S" and you probably better discuss it in detail.

"TALKING ABOUT SEX IS NOT ONE OF MY STRENGTHS. I PREFER JUST HAVING IT."

Yes, everyone knows sex is a huge part of marriage, but viewpoints between partners on the subject differ wildly.

Having a good sex life is essential to staying healthy, both mentally and physically. It's a basic component of a strong relationship. It is also a mutual act that should be shared freely and regularly. It should never be dictated, controlled, withheld or used as a weapon. When a major disagreement needs to be hashed out, couples should consider having sex before that discussion. This has been shown to completely change the way the discussion proceeds, and it can positively impact the outcome.

Sex is an undeniably powerful component and ally in a marital relationship. If you're having issues here, it's usually a red flag that there are major problems elsewhere that need to be addressed. Don't ignore the signs or sweep them under the rug. You likely won't renew your relationship at the end of the term if this basic need goes unmet.

So, how often? What do both of you need to keep things from becoming routine? Express everything, including fantasies, desires and romantic ambitions. **Also, state the stuff you don't like**. If there might be a major stumbling block in the bedroom, the sooner you deal with it, the better.

Get it out, write it down, and understand your partner's perspective in order to make the experience an active and healthy one.

What are the other expectations? What about recreation and fun? What about hobbies and special interests? Is he a traditionalist who believes she should prepare a home cooked meal a certain number of times a week? Does he see it as her job to wash, iron and fold the laundry? Does he have expectations for how clean the home typically needs to be? There may be a quick kiss goodbye after finding all that out, but then again maybe you get into some great discoveries you never would have thought about.

The point is that it doesn't matter what the couple agrees to.

It only matters that they BOTH agree, and that they spell out what they want and expect. You don't know if you don't ask. Don't think for a second your partner should just read your mind because, in reality, they can't.

Take the opportunity to define one another's needs. Beyond the basics of sex and flowers on holidays, get to the nitty-gritty: income expectations, household duties, fidelity, finances, kids, pets, mannerisms, daily routines, even how you will spend vacation time. Is it a requirement that you travel to Paris or Tahiti sometime during the course of the initial contract? Is a trip to the in-laws considered a vacation or an obligation? Should you have date night at least once a week? Etc., etc., etc.

Again, write it all down!

There's power in putting things on paper. Not only does it make them concrete and easier to communicate, but the process tends to clarify thinking. You'll start to see how things fit together, or you might become aware of areas where your expectations are inconsistent. Studies have shown that writing accesses a different part of the brain. The process has a tendency to elevate the discussion.

Imagine that this couple went through a highly detailed investigation of the things each of them perceives as requirements to a happy marriage. Consider what might happen if they were completely honest, even to the extent that they were willing to fight rather than settle for a situation they could imagine leading to resentment and eventual long-term conflict. What a huge benefit to understand each other's exact expectations.

What a step in the right direction to actually **become aware of their own expectations,** before the marriage commences!

This process has all sorts of side benefits.

First, it forces couples to confront the *deal killer* issues before they take their vows. It's possible that they will discover that they really don't belong together at all. What if he has a need that she's simply not willing to meet? Or she has a condition for him that he won't accommodate under any circumstances? You might as well know about that problem up front. On the other hand, things that seemed an absolute necessity may end up being trivial when discussed.

Second, they might discover things about themselves that they never really realized. Like before being confronted by his desire to move out of state, she might not have recognized she'd be unwilling to ever move away from her hometown. Probably need to know that before he takes that promotion to sales manager in Toledo.

Third, one of them might learn they can make their partner feel loved through a simple gesture. They might discover a way of connecting with this person that's more powerful than anything they'd ever imagined, and far less expensive than what they thought they were going to have to do to keep their mate happy.

Obviously, there's no end to the number of points that could be made here.

Opening a quality dialogue and communicating (conveying the concepts you hold in your head to your partner so that they understand them) is a highly effective way of moving any type of relationship forward, and a romantic relationship between two adults is certainly no exception.

Now, if either partner wants to earn a renewal, they should probably do a little more than the basics. If the idea is to entice the other person into wanting to sign up again at the end of the term, you'd better get doing some enticing. If our elected officials can find creative ways to earn votes when they really need them, you can, too.

A Term Limits marriage might make people think twice about that second helping of gravy for dinner and the extra two helpings of ice cream for dessert. Maybe they'll pass when it comes to taking up a bad habit, such as smoking.

For once in the history of marriage, couples are going to have to really think about:

- **What their spouse is thinking of them**

- **What they'll be thinking at the time of renewal**

- **The consequences for their actions**

- **The fact that renewal might not be very far away**

Define the consequences.

Ultimately each couple decides the severity of penalties for breaching the contract before the agreed upon term has ended. The penalties should be stiff enough to discourage casual non-compliance. This part of the process can also reveal how serious your partner is about their commitment. If they are requesting a three-strikes-and-you're-out policy for fidelity, for instance, it's a **red flag** that there will be problems on the horizon. Abuse ought to also be grounds for immediate termination of the contract. The fact that this is all predetermined greatly diminishes any shenanigans.

In a good contract, I see individuals actually becoming better people.

I see lots of people hitting the treadmill, bringing home flowers, going on dates and having "extra" sex.

Wow, imagine that.

It brings accountability into the equation on so many levels. Quite the opposite of what mostly happens in marriage today, after the ceremony is over. You know your term has an ending point and if you enjoyed the first term, you'll want a second and a third, etc.

So if you're at the point where you want to take it to the next level and totally commit, put your partner to task and agree to the parameters that are acceptable to both of you… not just one. Define your commitment. Define your needs. Agree to a length of time to see if those commitments to each other's needs will work. Define the consequences so you both know exactly what to expect if it fails. Always discuss how it's working with each other. At the end of the term, redefine everything, and do it all over again for the amount of time you both agree upon.

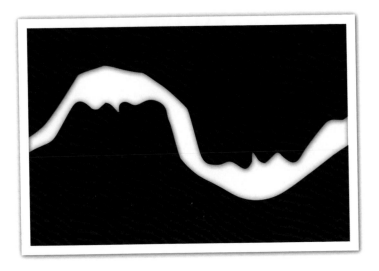

Stop Misrepresentation

The world is not black and white, right and wrong. We all know that.

But when it comes to being honest with your spouse, there are no shades of gray.

Things really are that simple. If you don't create any justifications to hide behind, the temptation to hide will decrease exponentially. If you're not telling your mate the truth, you're betraying them. **Conduct your committed relationships with this simple rule in mind. You'll be amazed at how much easier things become.**

Part of moving forward is closing the door on the past. If you need to leave it open, you're not ready to give what you need to give to someone who IS ready. For example, if you're still hung up on your ex, then get over them before you get involved with someone else and mess up their life. If you've become involved with someone but are still clinging to your past, be honest with them and don't misrepresent that you're ready to move forward.

Also, being single is different from being committed.

The behaviors and routines you had as a single person are great, and may have even introduced you to the person you're currently with, but continuing that behavior will have the opposite effect. Some of your single behaviors probably need to go away. Again, if you're not ready, then just don't pretend you are by trying to move forward with someone who is ready.

There are some misrepresentations that many people allow themselves to underestimate. **If you're still using internet sites to flirt or stalk or stay in touch with potential matches, you're probably not ready for a Term Limits relationship**. At the very least, you're not properly positioned to put in the commitment to make this new relationship successful.

Each of us knows how we are behaving on the internet, so if it's not good, stop doing it. If you can't change your behavior, don't pretend you can.

Be honest with yourself. That's the first step to being honest with others.

If you're still checking out your little sister's friends on Facebook and sending them flirty messages, you probably shouldn't be thinking about long-term commitments with your partner.

Facebook itself is an anomaly. It's a site designed around hooking people up. It gives them a way to check each other out without the social stigma of actually being on a dating site. It can be fun and informative, but can be used deceptively.

"THIS WEBSITE IS SO GREAT FOR STAYING IN TOUCH."

"I LOVE THIS MAGAZINE FOR THE ARTICLES."

Would you allow your spouse to be active on a dating site after you were married? Of course not, but hey, Facebook is okay, right? The reality is it's not much different than Match.com, when you get down to it. It's just less overt and more socially acceptable. At least people on Match.com are open about what they're there for. Again, just be honest with yourself about how you're using these sites. Facebook has a lot to offer, but there are real dangers if you're in a committed relationship. It has ruined many relationships. The smart move is to close the door on the past and get rid of anything that might interfere with your goals.

Maybe it's time Facebook created a new merged relationship status for couples! It would sure help protect marriages! If either partner could search the history and see their mate's chats, private messages, pokes (BTW, pokes? Give me a break!) and other information, people would be a lot less likely to take the first step onto a slippery slope that undermines their relationships. Hey, share how you feel about this stuff. Feedback is welcome at www.TermLimitsMarriage.com.

Scenario: Bob joins Facebook saying, "It's just a *friends* and family site where I can post photos for those I'm close to and get updates of how little Johnny is growing up."

Yes, it can be all that, but it doesn't take long until Bob comes up with an idea. He becomes friends with Heather with the ulterior motive of meeting one of her friends who he saw at a party but couldn't approach because of the unfortunate presence of her husband. On Facebook he can get a good look at her. **In fact, he can begin to develop a relationship that nobody else even knows about.**

Remember, he who lives by the sword dies by the sword. Even in the best case scenario, if you start a relationship this way, you'll always wonder what your mate is doing on Facebook or other internet sites in the future.

Relationships that are open and honest from day one are far more rewarding. It drastically limits the looking over your shoulder you'll always be doing if things start out sneaky.

IF YOU'RE NOT READY TO GIVE YOUR EMAIL AND INTERNET PASSWORDS TO YOUR MATE, YOU'RE NOT READY FOR A TERM LIMITS COMMITMENT.

Hooking up, lying, and cheating. There's an old saying that once a cheater, always a cheater. However, hooking up? I'm good with that. Regardless of my personal beliefs, I'm not going to pass moral judgment on anyone who is looking for nothing more than the physical. But geez, don't lie about it. Hooking up for sex happens all the time, but the real problem comes when you lie and cheat to accomplish it. Misrepresenting that you want a relationship when all you really want is sex is not okay. Again, being honest is a big part of being happy and having peace of mind. Not telling someone your marital status so you can get some action on the side is extremely damaging to all involved. Liars and cheaters are not good.

What's wrong with being honest? If you just want a hook up, surely there are plenty of others who want the same thing, so why not be open about it?

Why be deceiving?

If you're married and need that, then you probably didn't properly define your needs to your partner, or they failed to give them to you. In either event, talk it out with your spouse and fix it. If it can't be fixed then get unmarried first before hooking up elsewhere! I don't think hooking up between two consenting adults with honesty is the issue, but cheating totally sucks.

Lying and liars are a big problem. Get that out of your life. In fact, one of the main reasons for Term Limits is to stop people from lying… both to themselves and to others. When you get down to writing the nuts and bolts of your agreement, you'll start to see if your mate is sincere. Just the act of writing the contract will often expose those **representing** they are capable of doing things they are not.

You can't build anything on a lie, especially a relationship!

If you do lie, then there should be consequences! It's not okay. When you detail the consequences, you see what's at stake. Those who can't commit… won't.

There are all kinds of lies. Blatant lies, malicious lies, white lies, even lies we don't consciously think about.

Speaking of misleading promises, currently at weddings we hear brides and grooms make their vows blah, blah, blah then say...

"Till death do we part."

This is the part of the current marriage obligation I have the most trouble with. Seriously? You're sure you can do this until death? That's probably the first lie of marriage, and no one even thinks about it when they say it. You don't really mean, "Until death do we part," but because of the *fairytale*, most people stand there and recite the words.

Fortunately there aren't any actual executions taking place in divorce court, so you're safe... if you think divorce is safe. But why make the promise at all if you don't actually mean it? Now you might be thinking, "It's just ritual and ceremony," but there's more to it than that. It's a misrepresentation to everyone present at the marriage ceremony because you're vowing to do something you're really not sure you can do.

So why are those words the only choice we have to say at the altar when most people can't uphold them? That's how hypocritical this institution has become. There are so many things you don't know that you have to know before you could make a promise that epic. Even silly misrepresentations matter because they can subconsciously promote things that aren't going to happen. That's why I see Term Limits being so much more realistic. You don't lie about what's to be expected. Instead you make realistic promises that are bound by a time frame.

One more type of misrepresentation should be discussed. Many couples try *living together* to "test things out" before taking the marriage plunge. They expect it to be like being married with none of the hassles. There's an easy out if it doesn't work. This is very popular with a lot of couples these days, and who can blame them? But with no commitment, it's more like playing house. It's not the real thing. Don't kid yourself.

How many times have you heard of couples who lived together for years, got married, and then were divorced within months? Why? Because their live-in relationship wasn't binding. They tiptoed into something you should not tiptoe into. Sooner or later you have to face the fact that you have to give each other certain things, and be held accountable for doing so. As stated earlier, cohabiting prior to marriage has been statistically proven to fail at a greater rate than marriages in which couples did not cohabitate.

A Term Limits marriage is entirely different. There's a commitment and a term to which you agree to fulfill your partner's needs. You've made a defined promise to your mate that can be *evaluated and achieved*. These performance measurements keep both of you trying to enrich the experience for each other in order to fulfill the bargain you made. If you're not making a commitment, why pretend? Just date.

Internet Dating &
Compatibility Tests

Many dating sites include a form of the initial phase of the Term Limits contract. I'm referring to the *matching* or *compatibility* questions that they ask their users to respond to. The multiple choice questions range from extremely generic to highly personal. They cover the gamut from gender, sex, ethics, lifestyle, religion, family, habits, body type and politics.

Not only do the participants answer any questions they're interested in, but they also indicate which answers they would find acceptable from a mate. Additionally, they rate the importance of receiving a matching answer from the other person.

For instance, the user might be faced with the following question:

Do you smoke?

- ☐ Yes
- ☐ No
- ☐ Maybe

Responses you will accept:

- ☐ Yes
- ☐ No
- ☐ Maybe

How important is this question to you?

- ☐ Critically important
- ☐ Very important
- ☐ Somewhat important
- ☐ A little important
- ☐ Irrelevant

Etc., etc . and on and on...

These sites have developed formulas that take into account the importance of each answer in order to determine whether two people are compatible or not.

Obviously, a formula like that can easily miss a lot of subtleties, and it would have no way of predicting that a certain woman who is strongly repelled by smoking might somehow be able to accommodate that behavior in *one particular man*. There are many ways this couple might be able to work this situation out, but the important thing is that by asking the question they are forced into having an honest discussion of what those solutions might be.

The deficiency on dating sites is that they only use their questionnaires to help you make a match.

Why stop there?

Term Limits uses these questionnaires

at the point of making up your contract,

AFTER you've already chosen your mate.

Term Limits is not at all concerned about compatibility. You already decided you'd like to be with this person. Term Limits is focused on discovery.

Internet dating, itself, is a whole other story. As with anything there are problems. Their job is to find you a match and that's about it. If you're compatible then great, and good luck. Enjoy your match and we'll see you in a couple years... or months.

Congrats on finding your soul mate on HappilyEverAfter.com! We'll see you again soon

Even on the best sites you still have to sift through a lot of profiles that may or may not be really representative of whom you're looking at. That's time consuming, and then you have to still actually meet the person and see if there's chemistry. Plus there's always that awkward experience that two minutes after your date begins you desperately want to find an exit. And then, of course, that's the one person who keeps calling you afterward.

Okay, so here's an idea:

Maybe dating sites could be improved to be more consumer friendly. They should have an option where you could do, for

example, *Facetime Speed Dating*. You get three minutes to see if there's interest. If they don't give you a number, then you move on. If they do, you set up a lunch or something.

Also, at the bottom of every profile there'd be a post where people could "rate their date." You'd just click on "reviews" and get the scoop on past boyfriend/girlfriend posts, and with each comment there would be a five star rating system for the overall experience, kind of like Trip Advisor or Amazon. That would make it fun!

"YOU'RE DISAPPOINTED IN ME? THAT MAKES NO SENSE. YOUR PROFILE SAID THE MOST IMPORTANT THING TO YOU IS A MAN WHO MAKES PEOPLE LAUGH."

In all seriousness, finding the right person is tough no matter how you do it. So maybe there should be a site and a book and a plan, designed around making that experience enduring and enriching and keeping people happy together once they've found each other...

Hmmmm.

You've obviously found the book. Now take a look at the site. At www.TermLimitsMarriage.com you'll find an array of tools custom designed to make your Term Limits marriage a success.

Listen, people do things differently, nowadays, than they did in the past. **You have to recognize that society now interacts in ways we never could have imagined just a few years ago.** Some if this is for the better, and some of it is not. But we can pick and choose. While this process is in the learning curve, we can use technology to enhance our relationships and increase their quality in ways that could be more powerful than in the past. It all may be a little overwhelming, but if you think, for example, internet dating is convoluted, take a look at the history of marriage.

The History of Marriage

I am really sick of people saying, "That's just the way it is and the way it's always been done."

Well, no it isn't!

Nobody can say for certain how the practice of marriage began, but it seems to have existed, in one form or another, in every human society on record. **The most widely accepted theory is that powerful men wanted exclusive sexual access to certain women.** Among other goals, they hoped to assure that they were the father of any children the woman bore. In exchange these men were willing to pay what they call a *bride price*. Men would also provide for and protect the women they purchased.

"I JUST GOT A NEW WIFE!"

Throughout history it has been common for close relatives to marry. A 2003 *Discovery Magazine* article estimated that 80% of all marriages in history have been between second cousins or closer. Polygamy has also been common.

The practice of stealing women for mates has been widespread throughout history. Though it may seem barbaric to us now, at times it was viewed as correct and positive behavior.

In many cultures wives were considered to be possessions.

"BY THE POWER VESTED IN ME THROUGH THE CONSTITUTIONAL AMENDMENT RESTORING TRADITIONAL MARRIAGES, I NOW PRONOUNCE YOU MAN AND PROPERTY."

Women have often had little or no say about whom they marry.

It's been common for marriages, especially among those of higher social status, to be pre-arranged, sometimes even before birth. These sorts of marriages have played an important role in strengthening alliances, creating social structure, and transferring wealth.

What has not been so common – until recent times – is the concept that "love" is central to marriage.

Many cultures eventually restricted sexual relations to married couples, sometimes upon penalty of death. Most religions have defined adultery as a sin.

For centuries, marriages were not sanctioned by any institution, but eventually that changed and marriage became central to religion. Early Christianity taught the concept that marriage ought to be a sacred ceremony performed by a bishop. Other religions began formalizing marriages as well. Some have taught that a man's soul is incomplete until he unites in marriage with a woman and they become one. Others even claim that marriage goes beyond death and into eternity.

The practice of wives taking their husbands surname originated in the 12th century. State sanctioned marriages didn't occur until the 17th century. It wasn't until the mid-1800s that civil marriages became a legal alternative.

In 1837, England began keeping a registry of marriages and requiring that citizens notify the government of their unions. This clearly demonstrates that government only began playing an important role in marriages in relatively recent times.

Another relatively recent concept is the permanent division of assets throughout marriage. In modern Europe and the United States it is essentially the couple's choice whether they comingle their possessions or not. This was not the case in the vast majority of cultures over most of history.

While divorce has been discouraged by almost every culture and religion, nearly all of them have procedures for accomplishing it. The principle of no-fault divorce, enacted by California in 1969, made it much easier to instigate divorce in America. By 1989, every state had legalized this concept. Divorce rates rose dramatically in response. This particular "fix" actually undermined marriage and made it worse.

These are by no means the only pressures that marriage is under. Society is continuing to change rapidly, and human relationships are transforming along with it. As a result there are currently many factions looking for recognition from the marriage gods.

So, not only has marriage evolved over time, but the pressures that will force it to continue evolving are clearly in place.

Even if it weren't for the miserable condition that marriage is currently in, it wouldn't be the proper role of government to tell citizens what sort of relationship they are required to be in. But given that our government's own studies state that, "*The statistics do not describe the probability that a first marriage will last a lifetime,*" it's simply hypocritical that the current marriage contract does not allow alternative solutions.

It is even more absurd that changing the verbiage in the marriage contract from *life* to a *defined term* is not officially recognized by the government, yet it is okay by law to instigate a divorce without cause at any time. That potentially sudden and chaotic method of dissolution is completely recognized and endorsed. Not sure I see the logic in that. It's double talk.

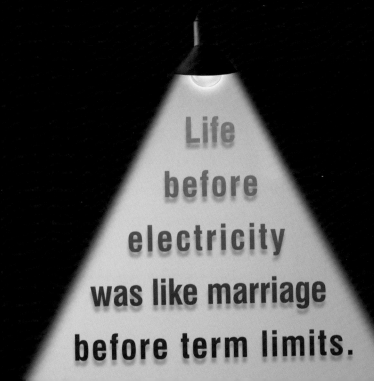

Life before electricity was like marriage before term limits.

Term Limits in Action

Personally I don't have a problem with just saying, "To heck with the current model." I think we need to do things that are right for our relationships and quit trying to conform to a broken institution with the life promise that few people respect or uphold.

It's time for action and an overhaul.

I'm not worried about getting everyone's approval before I do it. I'm not worried about what the current rules are for marriage. History shows that laws and customs always change when it's discovered they have outlived themselves. They will evolve when society has finally had enough.

If some people decide they want to stay with the rituals and ceremonies currently in place, then that's okay. *But why shouldn't the rest of us be able to choose options that better fit our needs?* Why should everyone have to go through the broken procedures we currently have in place in order to create relationships that don't endure? We ought to just commit to the one we love and marry them in the way we believe is best. **Shouldn't that be a personal choice?**

The government knows the current setup doesn't work, so why not change it? Why are we being forced to sign a contract, in order to be recognized as "married," that contains a universally applied *life term*, which can only be terminated through death or divorce? Why are there no written parameters? Why can't anyone even provide a meaningful definition of marriage?

WELL GUESS WHAT? WE DON'T HAVE TO PUT UP WITH THIS ANYMORE.

Term limits is the WAY OUT. You have to grasp the idea. I'm suggesting that, regardless of your current state law or anything else, we should all write our Term Limit contracts right now!

If you choose not to, that's okay, but don't worry if I do. And don't stop me. Every component in this book can be implemented today. We don't need to wait for someone to approve it!

However, because of the life contract you currently have to sign, a problem arises at the end of your term in a Term Limit contract, but only if you decide you want out. Dissolution will only currently be recognized by the state once a divorce is filed, approved and attached. So that's the part that needs to change.

Thanks to California's wildly popular no-fault concept, filing that divorce is no problem, even though living through it might be. Eventually the concept of the marriage being allowed to expire at the end of its term will make sense and become allowed by law without forcing anybody to go through this step.

When we renew, on the other hand, there is a technical glitch, but there are no complications. The state will not see that renewal as an extension but rather as **a continuation** under the status of their life marriage. Those are essentially the legal issues that people doing TERM LIMIT contracts would have to deal with.

So ultimately, if you:

1) **Incorporate a Term Limits contract into your marriage, today, with its specific parameters, duties, and performance expectations,**

2) **Tell your partner, "I'm giving you X number of years to prove we can enjoy a successful marriage."**

3) **Pre-set the terms of dissolution, regardless of what the state says...**

YOU'RE DONE!

You'll sign an extension at the end of the first contract if the relationship is still working for both of you, or you'll file a no-fault divorce and dissolve the relationship as prescribed in your Term Limits contract if either of you has chosen not to renew.

With one simple but major change to the current marriage contract, we could achieve a more workable agreement. Let's take out the "till death do we part" bit. It's time to put an end to that lie. At the same time let's remove the stipulation that only provides death and divorce as options for dissolution. We want to allow couples to put an expiration date on their agreement, just like anybody can specify the ending date of any other contract. With that change we could start working with each other, rather than working against the odds.

And why not? History proves we've modified this thing thousands of times. It's time to do it again.

THE VALIDITY OF THE TERM LIMITS CONCEPT HAS NOTHING TO DO WITH LAW. LAWS WILL NOT CHANGE TERM LIMITS.

TERM LIMITS WILL CHANGE LAWS!

Creating a Term Limits Marriage Contract

The peace of mind is worth it.

I propose we get back to the basics. Each of us knows our inner boundaries, our limits, our commitment level and what's inside our hearts. We know what we can realistically commit to! Consequently, we need to create agreements we can live with and adhere to in order be successful.

In doing research for this book, I was amazed to find how this movement is taking hold with likeminded people around the world. There is actually a lot of chatter going on related to this subject.

There are contracts already being drawn up in Mexico, Australia and Germany, and other countries probably aren't far behind.

I'm not going to make you read an actual contract, but here are the salient points that need to be covered.

First, at its core level this is a document that should be an expression of your love. Here's an example of how you might begin:

This agreement is made and entered by and between <NAMES OF BOTH INDIVIDUALS>. As individual people, we acknowledge mutual love and respect. In fact, it can and should be said that we adore each other right now and want nothing more than the happiness of each other. And for this singular purpose, we choose to make a commitment to each other that we will place the other's needs above our own and forsake the natural priority that we are given for ourselves, in exchange for the other's benefit for the following <TIME PERIOD>.

For the duration of this contract we shall love one another exclusively. We shall bind to each other and shall strive to further develop our relationship as husband and wife. We shall support each other in all matters by prioritizing the needs of the other above all.

Next we need to create the body of your contract, which should include (but not be limited to) the following sections:

Our commitments, needs, and desires, as well as our expectations and hopes, will be specifically set down for each to acknowledge, as stated below:

1) Effective date

2) Stated needs of each partner

3) Actions required to fulfill the needs

4) Interval feedback period – for example, once a month

5) Ability to modify the agreement

6) Right to renew

Now in order to protect both parties in the event of breach or termination, the following things need to be put in place.

We shall individually evaluate our level of satisfaction with this relationship on an ongoing basis. At the end of the term, in the event of a singular dissatisfaction, this agreement shall be deemed terminated. At that point we will agree to follow the rules of dissolution outlined in the sections below.

In the event of mutual dissatisfaction we agree to:

1) Property distribution upon dissolution specifically defined for each partner

2) Alimony

3) Early termination fees

4) Breach (for example abuse, criminal activity, or any activity you predetermine, as a couple, to be in violation of your contract)

5) Jurisdiction and state law when it comes to child custody

In the event that each of the parties to this agreement are individually satisfied, there shall be a renewable option at the conclusion of the term (specify time). At this point a fresh contract will be negotiated and executed.

Obviously a lot of important and very individualized information needs to be collected and entered into each Term Limits contract, but as you can see, the agreement itself doesn't need to be overly complex.

Investing this time and effort up front, though, can pay huge dividends for your future.

Getting Re-elected

You're three years into a four year contract when you recognize you made a smart choice for a partner and have a pretty great catch. The commitment you've shown by first signing the document and then keeping up your end of the bargain, is starting to make you realize you want to remain with this person long-term, rather than go play the field again once the Term Limits date arrives.

What can you do to convince your mate that they should re-up? It's kind of like running for a political office.

You think you've done exactly what you should've and she's going to automatically renew. Truth is, maybe she thinks she's made a mistake and is tired of your routine.

OOPS!

Refocus! Remember when you wrote down everything about each other and what you needed? What attracted her to you originally? Why did you get together in the first place? How did you start dating? Guess what. You have the answers. It's all there. You wrote it down!

Go back to the contract and figure out what's different. What changed for her? Fix it or take your lumps. Guaranteed you are not the guy she started with three years ago, so find out DURING your term how you're doing. Things change, so even if you think you're doing great, ASK her regularly. Change the bad and push the positives.

What can you do to make up for your shortcomings? **Similar to a politician who realizes his constituents aren't going to be particularly fond of a certain aspect of his voting record, you'll need to give your spouse a good reason to take the bad with the good.**

Fortunately, you know she's crazy about the ballet, and although it's not your favorite pastime, you've discovered that experiencing it with her does have certain side benefits. It sweeps her away into a fantasy land. She becomes a creature of passion anytime you go to the theater together. Yeah, season tickets to the Met were never anything you imagined purchasing before, but man, are you ever going to earn some brownie points once you present them to her. Again whatever it is, bring in something that is mutually beneficial and enriches being together.

But let's say your wife also decides that her preference would be to continue this relationship, and she might be straightforward enough to say, "Honey, I want to convince you to renew our contract. In fact, I'd prefer to do it sooner rather than later. I'd like to prove to you that you should want that, too. Is there anything you need from me to get us ready for the next term?"

Again, no games!

Being truthful with each other makes writing the renewal term even more fun. However, pointing out that she's gotten a lot fatter than her sister is probably not the kind of truth she's looking for from you. Besides being shallow, it ruins an opportunity for you to highlight the great stuff. Focusing on that gets you more of it. Having respect and good manners never goes out of style.

On the other hand, what if three years of marriage have made you realize that a lifetime with this person is vastly different than you had imagined it was going to be? Well, you've got a simple way out, and it's only a year away. There's no need to allow this situation to turn messy the way divorces traditionally do. The terms of the contract are clear. There's really no disputing who gets what when the relationship dissolves. It was all written into the agreement, just like any other contractual relationship that two parties might enter into.

"Sorry, Bob. You haven't kept many of the promises you made four years ago and my needs just aren't being met. Besides, you flirt with every girl you meet, and that thing you do with your nose hair really grosses me out. I'm afraid you're not getting that renewal."

Sometimes things don't work no matter what you do, and the relationship unravels. It's going to happen. That's okay. Be kind in departure. It's not the end of the world. In fact, oftentimes it's better to know as soon as possible and move on. But if it does come apart, **MOVE ON!** The back and forth thing is so debilitating and hard on everyone. Be kind and grateful for the time you had together, and look forward to the next chapter in your life.

Be glad your affairs
are already set so you
have one less thing to
worry about.

Avoid the Messy Ending

Did you read the title and immediately think, "Is there any other kind?" As I said before, it shouldn't be messy. Of course there are divorces that become a simple matter. Not all couples separate with animosity and lawyers.

Some couples are mature enough and healthy enough to end their marriage peacefully and equitably without going to court, even remaining friends and in contact with each other.

That's the way divorce should be if it has to happen.

Unfortunately, the success these people experienced in separating their lives had nothing whatsoever to do with the marriage contract. Why does that matter? Because if there had been some reason for conflict, the document they had believed was the basis for their relationship isn't worth the paper it was written on.

Not only isn't there a single clause in there that's going to help with the dissolution of their union, but the divorce system is actually set up in a way that's likely to increase (rather than decrease) conflict as these two people move forward in separation.

Marriages are failing at an alarming rate for whatever reason...distractions from the goal at hand, the rise of narcissism in social media sites, the constant barrage of sexual messages, lack of quality time together, etc., etc., etc.

So apart from those few who can separate peacefully when things unravel, there needs to be something better than divorce court to handle the break up.

"IT WAS TOUGH, BUT THE DIVORCE IS FINAL. HARRY'S LAWYER SETTLED FOR THE VACATION HOME AND MY LAWYER IS TAKING THE CARS AND THE BOAT."

Why can't a bad relationship just end if the couple has already prepared for it? If the marriage *term* date has been reached, no renewal is possible, and division of assets has been pre-determined, why shouldn't it be allowed to just *expire*? That's what advocates of Term Limits already ask.

Imagine a marriage contract that was designed to strengthen and support good marriages and also to help dissolve bad marriages.

That's what Term Limits is about. You have to sift through the garbage and get to the meat of your union.

Relationships using such meaningless agreements as the current marriage contract are priming themselves for failure.

They are based on futuristic pie-in-the-sky and hope-for-the-best stuff.

Written words will give you a guide to measure performance. They'll identify the reasons and truths behind being together and then help you understand whether the needs of the couple can be mutually satisfied before moving forward.

Actions speak louder than words when it comes to getting re-elected and measuring how enriching the experience was together. Words without actions are hollow. So having a specific predetermined term with dissolution already settled, in case a partner's actions don't match their words for whatever reason, prevents fighting it out later.

Should the relationship fail, you need to be moving on and not getting hung up going through – or merely surviving – a messy divorce.

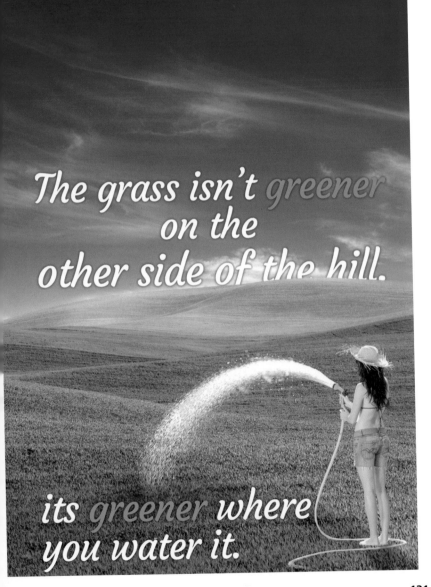

The grass isn't *greener* on the other side of the hill.

its greener where you water it.

Kids Are a Benefit

Healthy relationships create healthy families. The main reason that marriages are so important is because of the magical ability of men and women to get together and create new human beings. **Stable families are critically important to kids.**

Children born outside of marriage have diminished rights and status in many cultures, but despite this, in modern times the percentage of such births has risen dramatically. National Center for Health Statistics numbers show that births to unmarried women in the United States have risen from 30.1% in 1992 to 40.8% in 2010. Many countries are even higher, with Columbia being the extreme where 74% of children are born to unmarried women.

This is simply unacceptable.

New humans are quite unlike new versions of any other creature on the planet. For instance, a puppy is ready to leave its mother behind in about eight weeks. Even though there are seven dog years crammed within every human year, neither the mother nor the father dog are obligating themselves to anything very drastic if they decide to give puppies a try. There's no need to figure out who will drive to piano lessons or how to pay for college or where the money will come from to afford the weddings when little puppies grow up.

With humans it's a whole different story. Until you've created a human of your own, you really can't imagine the amount of work and the sorts of obligations parents face for years and years after the birth. You also can't comprehend the level of emotional attachment or investment that you'll have. The fact is, it takes at least eighteen years to properly raise a new human.

As a result of this math, something needs to be addressed when it comes to having children. In a Term Limits marriage, it would take most of five four-year terms to cover the period required to raise just one child, and if a marriage produces more than one kid, the number of terms necessary could become highly problematic... especially if one of the parties came to the conclusion along the way that they wanted to let their partner's option expire.

Technically, there is no difference in Term Limits marriages and traditional marriages because people go right on getting divorced, whether they have kids or not. In a Term Limits marriage, kids would create another important reason to want to renew. Custody laws and child support would still apply if you chose not to, so maybe before you have them, there should be a predetermined modification to the term.

This would be where an important aspect of the contract comes into effect, and it should be noted, this clause is a major reason why it is highly recommended NOT to have children during the initial term of the relationship. Now for some people who have moral qualms with contraception, this might create all sorts of hidden dangers related to entering into the contract in the first place, but the majority of modern couples have plenty of means at their disposal to ensure that young ones aren't popping out of the oven in an unscheduled manner.

So the unique aspect of the Term Limits contract that I'm referring to is known as:

The Eighteen Year Acceleration Clause

Having children should be a serious undertaking. If you're going to have kids, you better plan for them. That's the right way to have kids. It shouldn't just be an afterthought. If you're having kids to "save" your marriage, you're in the wrong relationship.

I'd say kids are a pretty great reason to want to renew your commitments, and they're a pretty good reason to want to fulfill your part of the contract. However, I believe it takes the commitment to a term of eighteen years together. Can you both do that? Be sure, because children coming from broken homes are always hurt by their parent's poor decisions. On that topic, here's something to think about:

Why is it okay to hurt children through divorce, but any other form of harming kids is considered child abuse?

Children are a potentially wonderful extension of the Term Limits agreement when two people have been through enough time together that they can comfortably say they are really ready for a major leap of faith. Nothing is better than a happy loving family.

By the way, get pregnant by accident and you just invoked the eighteen year Term Limit acceleration clause automatically.

Now, you might be able to get out of that contract, but it's going to be very expensive.

Even the current laws will see to that. You'll probably end up in court suffering through a traditional divorce. That's the exact thing you set out to avoid by putting your Term Limits marriage together in the first place. Think very seriously about the repercussions of sex without birth control or planning.

Wow, imagine how great it would be for all kids to actually have parents who:

- Planned for their arrival
- Stayed together
- Lived in the same house
- And were happily committed to the family

I'm not saying that everyone should have kids or even be together forever (thus the whole idea of Term Limits in the first place), but if they do, then they should live up to their end of the contract! It's far too easy to split up a family without the guilty party having any repercussions. What would your kids vote for? If you can't fulfill the contract then don't have them.

Kids are possibly the greatest gift of being in a loving, healthy relationship.

Other Term Limits Benefits

What is the point of having a relationship if you don't intend to have the best relationship possible? You're not getting married for marriage's sake! You should get married because you want to be with someone you believe can help you reach higher levels in an enriching partnership experience.

I believe in living life to the fullest with the right person or doing it alone until you find a mutually agreeable mate. I do not believe in doing anything halfhearted. Life is too short to settle for someone who won't give you what you need.

Speaking of needs, the core concepts that you've just learned about with Term Limits are also mirrored in concepts that help you elevate your life experience to higher levels.

The clearest way of saying this is to borrow from the *thinkers*. Abraham Maslow conceived of the hierarchy of needs. Though modifications emerged to his theories, his principals have stood the test of time. **He explains that it's almost impossible to reach the highest levels of the human experience unless you've already satisfied the basic needs that come before.** Take a look at his hierarchy as it relates to the Term Limits concepts:

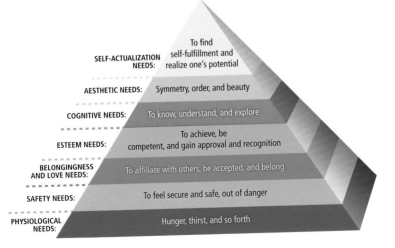

SELF-ACTUALIZATION NEEDS: To find self-fulfillment and realize one's potential

AESTHETIC NEEDS: Symmetry, order, and beauty

COGNITIVE NEEDS: To know, understand, and explore

ESTEEM NEEDS: To achieve, be competent, and gain approval and recognition

BELONGINGNESS AND LOVE NEEDS: To affiliate with others, be accepted, and belong

SAFETY NEEDS: To feel secure and safe, out of danger

PHYSIOLOGICAL NEEDS: Hunger, thirst, and so forth

If you're **hungry and thirsty** nothing else matters. You are on the lowest rung of the ladder. You will devote everything to simply getting your basic physiological needs fulfilled in order to survive.

Next comes **safety**. You can't move forward until you're safe. (Fighting with your mate or ultimately being in the midst of divorce makes you feel unsafe). The higher achievements in life aren't even in your realm. They are inaccessible because you're threatened.

Now take a good long look at the third need from the bottom:

Love needs.

More than half of the pyramid – and it's the good half, by the way – is inaccessible to us if we don't feel love. That's how important this is.

It is virtually impossible to reach your greatest potential, or to even come anywhere close, if you haven't satisfied the need to be safe and feel love.

Many live their whole lives just trying to get to the third level, only to get sideswiped by divorce and thrown down the pyramid. They struggle to find security and safety again because the crushing blow is actually a two-step setback.

Maslow believed that only after mastering each level could you move up the pyramid.

Accessing the vast majority of your potential is therefore contingent on getting your simplest needs met.

Your dreams are not at levels one, two, or three. Your dreams are at the higher levels. The fairytale exists **beyond** level three.

You don't have a clue about what you're missing if you're stuck in the doldrums at the bottom of the pyramid.

"BEAM ME UP."

More benefits that could be created:

If the government of a free society really wants to get involved with personal relationships, it should only do so in a way designed to produce positive results. Since it's been proven that *life* contracts for marriage are not working, why is that the only option? How about rewarding positive behavior that gets results instead? **Recognize and reward the things that diminish turmoil instead of rewarding divorce attorneys, who often create more conflict and prolonged suffering.**

Think of it like alternative energy solutions. People who come up with ways to use wind power or solar energy get tax breaks. I say we do the same for marriage.

Think of this. Because there would be less time spent in divorce court, a government subsidy could be paid to each individual who fulfills their term contract and even a bonus to those who renew. Maybe even an extra tax deduction for every five years for those who stay out of divorce court. **Term Limit marriages, if constructed correctly at inception, would definitely save on ridiculous lawsuits involving *he said/she said* contests. It would be all predetermined. Hey, if a marriage turns bad, no need for attorneys and divorce or taking up court time to settle disputes. The marriage just expires and each takes their predetermined assets and moves on.**

If it's good, you get a marriage tax incentive when you renew. Maybe there should be a substantial government incentive available to all couples who achieve the twenty year mark in their marriage. Even more for getting to thirty, forty, etc. It can't be that hard to turn this thing around.

Certainly the idea of pre-planning a marriage with the Term Limits concepts would have great advantages over marriages that just "hope for the best."

The odds are stacked against your never having to suffer through a divorce. That's your only option if you need to get out of a bad marriage (other than death). It's happening every day in America, and lots of good people's lives are being destroyed over the lack of discovery, pre-marriage communication and education, realistic expectations, and actually enforcing commitments. Why not do it right at the inception and put a time limit on it to succeed? If you don't think marriage is a contract... remember... you're wrong. Why make it a bad contract before you even get started?

If that's not enough to motivate you to figure out how to make these things happen, then add to the discussion. Open up dialog. Propose a better idea. We've set up a system on our website for doing this. Simply go to www.TermLimitsMarriage.com and click **Ideas**. Do something other than just allowing things to continue the way they are.

Wrapping It All Up

There's a reason for doing all of this that needs to be drilled into our very core.

LIFE IS SHORT!

It holds for us both highs and lows. It has so many fascinating, wonderful moments. These are moments that were meant to be shared with those who love us back and who want to share. **Your life can be all you dreamed it would be.** Find someone who you can love and who wants to love you. Make the mutual commitment to put forth the effort to make your life an enriching and rewarding experience together.

If you utilize these concepts, you'll realize quickly whether your partner is the love of your life or a learning experience along your journey. Always be positive and make choices that will ultimately bring you happiness. Being happy is not just a "state of mind."

Happiness takes work, conscious effort, and planning.

Time is precious. Term Limits has an ending point because time matters! You don't really have a lifetime to figure it out. Time is a predator that constantly stalks every one of us. Sooner or later it will catch up to us and our lives will be over.

With wasted opportunities comes regret. Regret and loneliness are sad bedfellows. These are not the partners we want to spend our lives with.

So how did you spend your time? My hope is that each one of us learns to spend our time wisely. We should avoid wasting time enduring and eventually dissolving a bad marriage. Or worse yet, force our children to endure a bad marriage and divorce.

If you never get married, that's okay, but if you're contemplating it or even if you're already married, take some time with your partner to plan what comes next. Do it right now. Ask them what they need from you, and tell them what you need from them. Write it down. Make real commitments within a defined term that you can easily reach and achieve, and never stop doing it.

Redefine your needs as they evolve, and enjoy this process with your partner.

Renew your contract over and over, and don't let today's silly distractions interfere with your chance at an enriching lifetime experience. Maybe it doesn't last fifty years, but I'll bet it does. Even if it doesn't, what you'll learn, no matter how short your time together, will prepare you for the partnership that will last.

These experiences will help you gather the freedom and wisdom you need to leave the wrong relationship for the one that will stand the test of time.

That's far better than the shattered fairytale of today's marriages, the majority of which end in bitter divorces that ruin lives.

We owe it to the lovers we make promises to, to our families and friends, to our neighbors, to our children, and ultimately to ourselves.

The time to stop this broken institution from disintegrating our society is now.

The people we entrusted to help correct marriage's woes decided to sanctify divorce instead. Until they are forced to, they won't change, so don't expect too much from them. Set things up correctly at the beginning of your relationship to give it a fighting chance of moving forward and lasting through time. Do it right now – TODAY – before tomorrow comes and your chance to change is gone. Do it before time catches up to you and you realize you wasted your opportunities to experience the love of a lifetime. Do it before the love of a lifetime walks away.

Listen, if you think I'm against the idea of marriage, you would be wrong. I'm against an institution that's set up so poorly that it fails more than it succeeds.

I'm against the way marriage is so easily dismissed and falls short of all the goals and expectations of the participants involved. I'm against the lack of planning and the devastation that happens to families once a marriage breaks up. I'm against the fact that it is so easy for one person to lie and manipulate another through the current marriage system with no consequences.

As a matter of fact, that person usually gains from their lies and often has nothing at stake when they break their vows and commitments.

"Oh gee, it didn't work... just get a divorce."

That's what we have now. **That's the current state of the marriage experience!**

For those who have succeeded, I salute you. Yet the facts show that you are in the minority… and it's getting worse all the time. Marriage is currently an undefined relationship at best. Its promises are vague and hollow.

What you will gain from an honest, defined relationship outweighs the effort it takes to define it.

You will have a much more enriching experience and a peaceful outlook. You will get to the heart of things quicker. You will know the terms and what's at stake if either of you break your part of the bargain. If you are unsure whether you'll actually get what you want, your defined relationship should be for a short term. At the end of each month, you should both discuss your progress. Both need to agree that each did their part. The first time that doesn't happen is when you know things need to be addressed.

Fix it and get back on track with the tools you used when starting out.

And remember. Nothing is ever perfect, but if it's clearly not working, getting out before it gets worse saves everyone's sanity. Be kind in your goodbye. Remember, a person who wishes you the best and pursues a course to being successful at happiness is far more attractive and healthy than one controlled by anger, fear and jealousy. The person controlled by these negative emotions destroys themselves and rarely hurts the feelings of the one their emotions are directed toward.

I really want to see marriages work, but they just don't the way they are currently set up. It takes more than just saying, "I do," at the altar. It takes effort, planning and meeting the needs of both people involved.

I want to see my daughter – healthy and in love – in a happy family where she never has to suffer the pain of a divorce and splitting up the time she will spend with her children.

Ultimately, I loved being married. However the pain and trauma that came with divorce left too many scars. Yet I truly think there's hope. We may need to rethink marriage like we have to think about voting for our elected officials. We have to get re-elected by our partners by fulfilling our promises to them.

If we lived our lives in marriage with committed, defined choices, upfront communication, realistic expectations and responsibility for our actions with enforceable consequences, we would all have a real shot at better relationships.

If BOTH partners have to tow the line and work together towards a goal, be it three years or fifty, I believe you'd find many more **relationships** evolving into long, happy **marriages**.

Many more couples would WANT to renew, and in that, re-commit to their partners for a more enjoyable experience. Those that don't WOULD NOT ANYWAY! Look at the divorce rates!

So don't kid yourself. Marriage as an institution is broken. It's time to face the facts and stop allowing this thing to flounder along, destroying the fabric of our society. **It's time for couples to live life on their terms.** It's time to get the fighting over with upfront, before signing the contract. It's time for planning and being responsible to your partner. It's time to tell the truth about marriage.

It's time for TERM LIMITS.

Epilogue

Mary looked down at Emily and after a long pause, she said, "You know, Emily, I have a better story to tell you. Life is what you make of it. It's like a big present that you give to yourself. When you open it, you get back all the things you put into it. It's always best to make sure before wrapping your present that it has all the things you know you want inside."